Gallery Books
Editor: Peter Fallon

A FURIOUS PLACE

Kerry Hardie

A FURIOUS PLACE

Gallery Books

A Furious Place
is first published
simultaneously in paperback
and in a clothbound edition
on 17 August 1996.

The Gallery Press
Loughcrew
Oldcastle
County Meath
Ireland

© Kerry Hardie 1996

ISBN 1 85235 195 0 (*paperback*)
    1 85235 196 9 (*clothbound*)

The Gallery Press acknowledges the financial assistance of An Chomh-
airle Ealaíon / The Arts Council, Ireland, and The Arts Council of
Northern Ireland.

Contents

for Seán and Will

'*I am the evil of the evil-doer,*
I am the pain of the sick,
I am the cloud and rain,
And I am raining in the meadows.'
— Rumi
1207-1273

We Change the Map

This new map, unrolled, smoothed,
seems innocent as the one we have discarded,
impersonal as the clocks in rows
along the upper border, showing time-zones.

The colours are pale and clear, the contours
crisp, decisive, keeping order.
The new names, lettered firmly, lie quite still
within the boundaries that the wars spill over.

It is the times.

I have always been one for paths myself.
The mole's view. Paths and small roads and the next bend.
Arched trees tunnelling to a coin of light.
No overview, no sense of what lies where.

Pinning up maps now, pinning my attention,
I cannot hold whole countries in my mind,
nor recognise their borders.

These days I want to trace
the shape of every townland in this valley;
name families; count trees, walls, cattle, gable-ends,
smoke-soft and tender in the near blue distance.

The Young Woman Stands on the Edge of her Life

1

Saying the words
mother, daughter, sister.
A trinity more dense
than *father, brother, son.*

Mother, the deep mud in the yard.
Daughter, a bowl,
a love-word, a receptacle.
Sister, stands beside me,
her sword drawn.

Where will I live?
Down here in the earth
with the women?
Or up on the hill where the dogs bay
and the men
feed watchfires?

The cleft stick jumps in my hand.
The path seeks
its own way.

2

Where they buried the rabbit they planted the hazel tree.
The earth dragged at the new roots
which parted the crumbling flesh as sweetly
as touch parts silk
soaked years in the sun.

It was all decided and accomplished
before she remembered that she had forgotten
to make her choice.

Where were we, Who were we, What was the Journey?

1

The ferry heaves, nudges the land back,
pushes to sea. We turn to each other,
butting our way into storm.

It is like growing
the shiny inside of an oyster shell. Nosing out
whorls and hollows; gorging valleys; flowing over
the smooth places. Later, when the flood tide drops,
the soft-bodied creatures that smell of fishes, of sea,
shrink and retreat. The shells lie out on the sands.

2

Inland in France the flowering grasses
were blowing and bowing themselves. They
were courtiers in watered silks: tawny and rose
with a pale nap stroked to the light
where the wind ran — a king's glance
conferring its arbitrary grace.

'The Fair Fields of France.' That lovely phrase
was in my eyes, over and over. It was green
and worshipful. It was a Book of Hours,
it was the covetous soul of Plantagenet England
honed with longing. I gave it like obeisance,
gave it like heart's tribute, never exacted.

And yet we left them. We left them
for the coasts, the Northern seas, the places
where boats rose on the tide and shells lay.

3

It always pleased him that the word for those
great horned shells from the warm seas was *conch*
meaning cunt. How they wound themselves
into their shining coral-red interiors.

For myself I loved the sea-journey.
How in the afternoon we sat by the rails and stared
at the vast, quiet glitter. Sometimes a gannet voyaging
the surface. Sometimes a ship far off by the horizon.

May

for Marian

The blessèd stretch and ease of it —
heart's ease. The hills blue. All the flowering weeds
bursting open. Balm in the air. The birdsong
bouncing back out of the sky. The cattle
lain down in the meadow, forgetting to feed.
The horses swishing their tails.
The yellow flare of furze on the near hill.
And the first cream splatters of blossom
high on the thorns where the day rests longest.

All hardship, hunger, treachery of winter
forgotten.
This unfounded conviction: forgiveness, hope.

Solstice

for Marie Foley

By a sliding river
to gather a quiver of feathers,
night reaching
far into day.

Mud and the gleam
of low light on mud.
Small mud-splashed bullocks
at the empty cattle feeder.

Rook, raven, hooded crow.
In the woods a ruckus
of wings; knave magpie
rattles and rules.

Arrow and flail,
hollow-iron twilight,
the gutting crow,
the fox at the ribs.

Nearer it draws, and nearer.
Feather of raven winging
the striped arrowhead
of our old-bone winter.

Now that She has Gone Away

She never liked pansies. *All those little faces,*
looking at you. I always made a point of sowing them.
When I left it late, I bought young plants in trays.
It was against my husband as well.
Not that he minded what flowers I grew,
but she was his mother:
it was my small gesture of defiance,
a staking of territory; mine, not hers.
He never noticed and I never told him.
He grows sorrowful when I reveal my jealous nature.

It is May now, and the first held sun of the year.
The pansies in the long box under the window
are straining to reach round the edge of the wall
and push up their velvet faces.
Every time I pass I feel their eyes following me.
Their plaintive yellow and purple and garnet gazes.
That's all she does now. Follows her husband around.
If I had it again I would open my heart and share everything.

In Time of Long Sickness, We Dream . . .

Three husbands I had, he said.
Himself; a thin man called Sickness;
a fierce man called Past.

Once I opened my hands
to let my life go
but they filled up with rain.

Now my hands are wide open,
spread like a butterfly in the sun.
Sickness and Past are flown from them.

The Husband's Tale

What is a wife?
            She sits in the car and waits
while he opens the gates, the roses on the wall
all blown in the rain which is fine and warm
and just greys the green of high summer
like the fine strands now muting her hair.
She will drive to the small country town
and park in the station yard
and stand at the grooved wooden window
and take the ticket and wait in the rain for the train
to Dublin, to the doctor . . .
                        And he thinks
how frail she is in her beige mac
in the green stew of roses and rain and birdsong,
how tired and quiet before the journey.
And he, in his strength, falters.
                        A loved wife is an underbelly
as soft and as stretched for the knife
as a frog's.

On Having to Stay Behind and Mind the Hearth

Sun out, wind up,
all the new chestnut leaves
racing into the morning.
Heart
chases after them.

Gone now. *Over the hills and far away.*
Into the spring, its green veils.

Heart never wants
to bide quiet here in its place again.
It knows something different now:
wilder, fresher, more abiding.

Heart, Heart,
let me go with you.

February Horses

The horses are moving
down through the gap, treading a way
from upper meadow to lower,
past the red barn

crouched in a pattern of branches;
five of them, chestnuts, one with a blaze,
hooves pulling against
the steady suck of mud.

They have been waiting up there
all through the night; now they straggle
the cropped and boggy pasture;
all beyond is shades of distance.

Nothing can quell
the leap of the eye seeing
the rhythm of bone and muscle under the mudded coats,
the long manes in the stripping wind, the pooled eyes;

and nothing can quell the gravitas of awe that they impart
to the thin, dark morning,
lights burning, the sediment of long defeat
stored in the bone.

These Daily Dramas of Emigration

The slowing thump of the train —
three sisters on the platform,
their heads stamped
on the cruel green coin of the spring fields,
one with a travelling bag
and short aubergine-dyed hair,
black trousers, black boots, black
jacket, a clean face broken open,
closed shut again,
not so young anymore,
going again anyway,
and we could see at a thrown glance
she was not going to make it.

With our eyes practised on emigration
we could see more than that. We could see
how she must have made them suffer,
especially when the first husband
was brought home
and settled for.

The two of them walking
beside the train as it moves away,
waving, holding tight to
the stretch-armed child strung between them,
their long, undressed, mouse-gold hair caught
at the nape of each neck,
the older fatter
and in some sort of anonymous skirt,
the younger thinner
and in jeans,
their eyes anxious
and righteous,
not wanting her gone,
wanting her gone

and behaving badly somewhere else,
everyone down the whole length of the train knowing
that when it has left they will turn their faces
back to the greening fields
and attend to their lives again.

The Localness of Weather

The dust came in the rains on the last day of April
to spatter the white plastic chairs
set out the day before and lying now
face-down in saxifrage and pansy.

We looked at its red stains on the white chairs,
thought of the Bible, the rain of blood,
felt superior to all that superstition,
turned on the news to be sure.

I stood out under the white windy sky,
suddenly full of house-martins and swallows,
saw they had been bundled up
in a Sahara dust-sheet, bowled to us

all the way over the lands and the seas from Africa
and shaken out into that piece of the sky
that seems, although constantly on the change,
to inhabit the above-of-us. Some Ancient of Days

providing swallows for sky, spattered red stains
for chairs, sills, white petals of tulips.
Contradicting the particularness of our landscape.
Marking small earth with great earth's blood.

The Farm Girl Remembers Home

for Heather

She spoke of that birthday,
of stories, one on another,
leaf drifting on leaf.
She spoke for a lost life,
for her own heart's yearning
now that she lives
outside the walls.

She spoke as one looking
on night-starry skies
when we are grown leaf-thin, violable,
and the high dreams float about our heads
and press through our waking selves;
her eyes, helpless and rapt,
watching herself dissolve.

What was she, only a country girl
in city trappings,
the gee-gaws in her ears
his fairings given her in some Glasgow bar?
Taking the pins from her crowned head,
letting the hair fall loose,
she could have been anyone's 'Brown Colleen,
the star of the County Down'.

It wasn't a happiness that had been,
and now was lost, in a city full of cries.
Only the bright squared quilts
spread airing in the yard.
The rest was tear-trails
down an ashey childhood.
It was a longing for her place,
to know her task, fend off this loneliness.

I was that, too;
I wanted to go back behind the walls
where I had lived and never lived,
to be again the peaty loam
and listen, sodden through womb ears,
to ancient dark-brown dreams,
leaf singing unto leaf,
stained water to stained light.

All Night I Coughed

Sometimes
I stood wait by the window,
watching the shine
of the lambing lights
in the valley. Sometimes

I boiled kettles — potions
mulled from herbs.
Sometimes out there,
the book open in my lap,
earth and sand falling out of it,

brown bits of twigs
sliding after them,
discoloured flower-heads
buckling the pages, the names
yielded themselves:

Skullcap, angelica,
mullein, red clover,
horehound, borage.
Sickness:
its ancient practice.

And all the time
the flared blackness
of pneumonia's bombed dreams,
the farm lights, the fever,
the solitary watch —

and in the morning, in the light,
I was fish,
intent,
swimming my way through darkness
towards night.

Ship of Death

for my mother

Watching you, for the first time,
turn to prepare your boat, my mother;
making it clear you have other business now —
the business of your future —
I was washed-through with anger.

It was a first survey,
an eye thrown
over sails, oars, timbers,
as many a time I'd seen that practised eye
scan a laden table.

How can you plan going off like this
when we stand at last, close enough, if the wind is right,
to hear what the other is saying?
I never thought you'd do this, turning away,
mid-sentence, your hand testing a rope,

your ear tuned
to the small thunder of the curling wave
on the edge of the great-night sea,
neither regretful nor afraid —
anxious only for the tide.

Sick, Away from Home

for Jean Valentine

1

In the first flat I lay in bed, watched
the plane trees, their slow leaf-drift, the screen thinning.

In Ireland it was harvest still, the trees solid with leaves,
but a dry rattle, morning and night, when the winds blew.

2

This flat: roof-windows onto the sky;
the press of its pale eye against the glass.

3

A woman's voice in the room beside me.
Restrained, well-bred,
she speaks of the laying of carpets.
Footsteps. The scrape of a drawer.
I see her, thin and fairish, in her middle thirties.
I lie here, listening for her,
but she does not come again.
A tap runs where my left hand rests.
A man says he will feed the vine.

Her voice being as it was, I put on make-up when I get up.
Half-moons on their backs below my eyes.

4

Wakeful in the very early mornings
I let the walls form themselves
in blocks and planes. There is no such colour
as white. Sometimes rain falls on the sky-windows.
Sometimes birds' wings and the flighting of pigeons.

You can twist the blinds,
make them roof or sky.
The chancey sunlight sifts through slats,
corrugates the wall with stripes.

Secret days. Unknown to anyone.

5

I can feel the ground going
from under my feet.

This is a place
for the fairy-tale rule of three.
The bad bits
blacken before redemption.

And everywhere — on white sills, ledges, shelves —
a film of dust, laid down by the fall of air.

The Return

for Fiona Brooks Ward

When I came back alone to the house
it wasn't the same.
Not only the birds
that I nudged off paths,
or the flowers that stood
privately giving birth to themselves,

it was something more,
something to do with
its not being separate from itself;
not being the object
of anybody's care or scrutiny,
nor sheltering anyone.

It just *was*. Like an old house,
fallen in. Attentive. Still.
Lilac growing over the empty doorway.
Blackthorn at the gable end —
its fruiting of blue-black sloes,
the dense air caught on its thorns.

And I thought, is that what we are like?
Our own selves,
unregarded?
Do we stand somewhere,
as secret, sufficient, fierce?
And burdened with fragrance, like lilac?

The Hunter Home from the Hill

Quiet by the window of the train
watching the blanched skies, the bleaching stubble,
a breaking down of colour
to something matte and porous and not at the heart of vision —

watching the winter lying down in the fields
as a horse lies — bone following bone —
the long ridge, the sheep, the blue note of the beet fields,

the bungalows on rutted patches starting awake
out of wild dreams in which they are gardens,

Carlow, the ugly here and there of it, the damp-stained houses,
the sky over the beet plant sausaged with fat round smoke,

all as it is,

like watching him in the kitchen in the morning,
his vest, his thinning slept-in hair, the way he is in your life,
and you content that he be there.

Siblings

The Derryman told of the childhood holiday in the village in Donegal and how he had gone with his father and caught a fish and had carried it home through the blue evening; and the pride of it, greeting people and them knowing, and his mother ready at the stove to cook it. How they had eaten the fish and it had lived inside him for years and years, as Jonah lived in the whale, only the other way round, and then when he was grown with a son of his own he went back to the village and there was no river in it or near it or flowing past it, no river at all.

1

There was a fish but no river
there was no river so there was no fish
there *was* a fish whether or not there was a river
and if there was a fish there *must* have been a river —
and anyway there was the blue evening
not to mention his father's hand on his shoulder.

2

We are always there, you and I, at the table
leaning forward, our elbows together
and our feet braced, our hands locked
and our eyes locked, and I do not know
any of the people crowding dimly
around us as we sit, implacable
at the fulcrum of our clasped hands,
ready at any moment
to force down the other's arm.

We argue, my brother, of fishes, of rivers,
yet you have pulled fish and I have pulled fish
thudding onto the bank, heaving, shining,
from the river that was no river.

Redemption

for Joan

On the morning of his death
he dressed formally,

then he sat in a chair with the paper, waiting.
It was all fear. And hard effort.

He had left off daily praying,
was too busy at dying to be praying.

After, she left off going to mass.
It had let him down somehow —

anyway, it clearly wasn't as he'd thought.
She had wanted to let him down herself,

but loving him, had waited till after.
So here we were in Cork, buying drisheen

because he had taught her a taste for it.
Sheep's blood, blended with milk, she said;

it would have been his birthday had he lived.
She could have been looking

into a spring well, the water so clear
you mightn't have known it was there:

a quiver of light when the wind rocked,
sweet to the tongue.

A Childless Woman

With young women I am motherly,
with older women, daughterly,
with women of my own age, lonely.

1

First a landscape smudged with sound
and trickles of sound.
Air threaded with rain.

Where the swollen river has loosed its brown waters
into the marsh-places
and the shine of the cold sky shows in flatness of flood —
there the frogs grunt,

heave, flop about in watery eruptions,
stilling when they hear us,
but for an old bull, quivering, out of his head with sex,
who regards us balefully from his station
on a female, submerged
in the spawny glub and not protesting.

It is all woven — woods, sounds, light;
before the frills and flutterings begin.

2

I have a part-time, not-mine, son,
loaned from a woman that I never meet.

Sometimes I wonder if she thinks of me.

3

It's no big deal, happens over and over.
Just haunted, in spring, by the slow file
of the grey women who have made me.
And I am them, and I am breaking the line.
This is what it means: the year the spring didn't come.
Spilled water, seeping underground.

A fragile time, February going into March.

4

I am become a woman standing on the sidelines,
on station platforms meeting and seeing off trains,
casually surprised to be remembering
with gifts the anniversaries of friends' children.
A woman given
to speaking carefully, saying mostly the generous thing,
watching the brown flow of rivers,
waiting by windows open to the dusk.

Red Houses

for Frances

There are in this country, off small roads in darkness,
certain red houses.
Not the red of blood but the red of fire:
red from the red women who live in them.

I have been in one such house.
There was nothing special, nothing to show.
The wooden gates stood open, the dogs were in,
and on the raw concrete step a bicycle

sprawled on its side in the thick black night air
that laid its wet finger to my face. Inside
the dark-haired red woman-of-the-house
stood by the table, pulled all eyes to her, and it was not

what she said, or did, or looked like, but the place
she drew her life from (some old ferned well
whose whereabouts I did not know) which so tuned her
that she glowed the house.

Fear for the children of such women,
especially the sons. For if they miss
the moment when it might be possible
to make the thing over again

they will spend their lives searching
through people and countries
and nowhere will they find again the red house
with the red heart in the soft black rainy night.

Five O'Clock Strand

for Pat Murphy

You sit in the grass, eyes closed, hands wrapped around your
    knees,
playing the game of 'What do I hear', hearing the sunny
    stillness,
the plate moved on the drainer in the house behind,
the two girls on the stones above the sands —
their fidget of shifting stones, their quiet talk, their laughter —
the dog inland — his few barks — the bee strayed from the
    clover.

The five o'clock news — its first unguarded sentence —
the lazy sound of the sea not even trying,
the fizz of the drying wrack, the wash of the silence.
You open your eyes; the fineness, the stillness, the glitter,
the man who walks the child up the grassy road,
the sea-grass, the tide far out, the absence of treachery,

the starlings fanning out across the sands.
It reminds and reminds of life's base sweetness,
of summers past, of summers not yet lived,
all our small lives, how they are given to us, how we accept
    them,
soft bellow of the cow behind the strand,
a time of day for milking and for tea.

Autumn Cancer

i.m. Liz Suttle

Each day, the autumn, eating a little further
into the bone.

A leaf falls on a stiller day, coloured a richer brown,
more glowing, more holding, like glazed bread or old apples;

and the lap of the lake gone smaller, a nibbling as of fishes
at feet in tidal pools. The heron stands longer.

Shoals of leaves float further on the water,
the low sun pulses, and light shafts pick more delicately

over woodland and the limbs of ash grown sensuous,
shapely, as a woman from a bath;

while on the alders, yellow, and here and there,
a round leaf hangs, spent coin in the stillness.

I have never known so exactly
this abacus of days. This withdrawal. This closing out.

Listening to Tolstoy

There is a lump on her left leg.
In the night she lies awake
and thinks about its shape.
Then she reaches down
and is amazed how small it is.

She hears the voices on the radio:
'How does one face death, Gerassim?
What does one do?'
'Nothing. It will all be done for you.
Even the fear will be dealt with
one way or another.'

There is a moment then
as after weeks of rain
seeing a stretch of sky
slung between two hills,
rinsed and cold and thinned as winter washing.

Arcanna

for Pat

He said he loved
untold secrets,
their iridescence;

how you shrank,
they shrank,
when you unfolded their maps.

Magpie, he said,
is a garrulous bird
that gobbles secrets.

Rogue magpie,
low in the thorn,
delirious with discretion,

swells and swells,
beats his drum, flicks his tail,
never tells.

Himself, he said,
he was close
as an oyster making pearls.

Interlude

for my father

My father told me how he dug up war graves,
picking out thigh bones — two per person — more accurate
than skulls which got mislaid and dumped.

I live in a house in a space in the fields.
This time of year we wake to swallows winging round the
    bedroom;
earwigs and woodlice garrison dropped clothes,
mice quarry soap, harvest-spiders occupy all ceilings.

The house is quietly invaded. He puts down peas and beans;
I watch the fragile blossom of the cherry trees,
the distances smudge-blue, the mountains floating.
Sniff the green rain, mourn every passing,
greet each shoot until they are so crowded and so many
I cease recording and admit the summer.

Lives. Theirs, ours. Human times are mostly hard.
They will be so again. Some veil, insubstantial
as wound-gauze, separates this from that.

Kilmalkedar Church, County Kerry

Unmortared stone. Uneasy weather.

A knot of calves lain in the grass —
black and white, not long born —
the ruined church with the roof that was built out of stone,
foreigners in waterproofs in primary colours.

Purple loosestrife, purple thistles,
the red-tipped darkness of the fuchsia hedge,
little fields that run down to the sea,
dun wrens, a twelfth-century priest's house, its two rooms,

the spring well by the door, the pale damp day.
And I think did some scribe see
calves laced like these, for his text?
What was the topography of his faith?

What was his weather?
Can we be measured in the lives
of past believers?
Is it for this that we clamber the fallen stones,

then stand, the inspection done, the visit unfinished?
For something still lurks of them here,
some gleam in the day,
a snag of prayers in the grass, a half-remembered threading

of men and women along the thin path
from the church by the shore
to the church on the hill's green shoulder.
Vigil, informed by the whiteness of daylight,
ice to be broken at the well on winter mornings.

And I know we can never be still or simple enough
for what they have left behind them:
a small strong vision snarled on a net of fields.

The Avatar

Listen, this is the trinity, he said, tramping the wet road
in the thin well-being of a winter morning:
God the curlew, God the eider,
God the cheese-on-toast.
To his right a huddle of small blue mountains
squatted together discussing the recent storm.
To his left the sea washed.

I thought it was whimsical, what he said,
I condemned it as fey.
Then I saw that he meant it; that, unlike me,
he had no quarrel
with himself, could see his own glory
was young enough for faith still in flesh and in being.
He was not attracted by awe

or a high cold cleanness
but imagined a god as intimate
as the trickles of blood and juice that coursed about inside him,
a god he could eat or warm his hands on,
a low god for winter:
belly-weighted, with the unmistakable call
of the bog curlew or the sea-going eider.

Colours

for Helen

'There is a blue, the signature of well-being.'
I read this of the Impressionists in the book that lay beside me
when the sickness was on me again like a shroud.
What blue? I never saw it in all this time,
no, not in the slate of the sea
nor in the grey-blue ink-weather days of the short year
pressing in over the white house with its two bright places
of candle and fire. Then, because it was Stephen's Day,
I got up and he took me out into the low murky light
with the rain in it. The colours of the land came up
jewel-strong, the purple in slates and stones by the grey sea
bloomed in my eyes, orange smouldered in weed.
And on the hillside the dead bracken
lay soaked and dark, dark red like old rubies that gleam in
     the rain.
A seal's head showed black in the bay.
                                        Inland the wrens
crept the dun hedges. Friesians crowded behind
the gable-end of the white-washed barn,
its fresh-painted gutters, sky-blue
and too thin a colour to echo deeply.

Spring Race

for Chris

The chestnuts have it.
One before all the rest
in that line of twelve
where the road swings by Foley's farm
has hitched limp green rags
to every spiked twig it owns

and the rags lift,
thicken in moist light,
fan upon fan. Translucent
as new ghosts, they own no shade.
Beyond, the spread corduroy of spring plowing.
And lambs shouting into the morning.

Late Spring

The pike is in the meadow by the river.
He makes furious rushes. You can see his path gouged
upwards onto the flatness of the flood.

Last year when the flood rains came
dandelions stared up through water.

The pike hunts frogs.
Child's play. Frogs
that should be flopping in flowers, practising themselves:
their mottled gold and black, the greenish patches,
the *pulse pulse pulse* of their underthroats
where the life runs too near the light.

Like the pike.
He may drain back to the river with the spate.
Or lie out in the meadow, bird-stripped bones,

the dandelions open, small suns on a green flag.

Enchantment

for Ruth Carr

In spring we open all the doors.
The wrens from the stone wall,
mistaking this for that,
cling helpless to the Indian curtains
faded and patterned
with birds and beasts
and flowering trees.

I'm fearful they will stay too long,
grow jaguar-spotted,
jewel encrusted,
their low brows sprouting
rich, embroidered plumes
that cannot be unwoven
from the muslin garden.

Those Old Ascetics

for Susan Watt

On Skellig Michael we sat down
among the haunts that thronged the place.
We listened to the guide.

We were so modern, all of us,
our cigarettes, our cameras, our trainers;
trousered women, sporting darkened lashes.

Squatting inside their domed stone huts
we stared through doorways into light,
searched the cut shape of the pale sea for reasons.

We marvelled at them, how they'd seek out
stone to lay their heads on,
fish bones and the bones of birds

for food. And in the mornings, always,
over and over, the same rests for their eyes:
sea-samphire, water, sky.

For their part, they didn't mind.
And they knew the men
that ran the boats that brought us here.

She Goes with her Brother to the Place
of their Forebears

— St Lazerian's Church of Ireland Cathedral, Old Loughlin

I have a lean, long-boned spite in me
against my religious lineage, the rites expected of me —
a spite that is satisfied here in this ruining Cathedral
with its frustration of all those aspirations
of churchmen and congregations.
I don't know what this is bred of —
what unknown disappointments, abuses, expectations
bubbling through the unreflecting blood —

but here where our forepeople gathered
I sense it is in you, too; that your easy limbs ambling the
    graveyard
may have coiled in them a derision waiting for its excuse;
that you have noted it is as a great ship
moored in a harbour silted up hundreds of years ago;
that now there is no chapter, close, school, town, city;
no bishop, deacon or vicar; just a long, narrow, thirteenth-
    century
stone barn; plainer than any Meeting House; in use.

Still, I was caught by your glee when I told you
that these forebears of ours were most likely Cromwellians —
Better than Huguenots, you said. I knew then
how you thought to sit in a pub with some friend
who had shifted his name into Irish, was blowing
about the Celticness of his home twilight.
Then you'd drop that word into the quiet; watch him
blink, shuffle, smile at you kindly: accepting, forgiving.

And how it eases something in me to see you so ready
to embrace the disgrace and crow from the still-smoking
      dunghill.
I lay my hand flat on the sun that lies on a webwork of lichen
crawled over a tilted slab. We watch the goats cropping,
the celandines blinking. Around us the graveyard
is steep with the dead. We stroll up the road in the sunshine
to seek out the well, the spring of the matter, the reason
for all this arrangement of stone, for the monastery buildings
      before it.

It's all railed-in, tidied and tended. The water
sleeps safe in its concrete box and flows
from a neat pipe by a sound drain in a mown lawn.
Beech twigs lay lace on the sky, there are evergreens, various.
And a small, worn stone cross on a plinth where a virgin
      stands.
Ancient. Not as ancient as she. Nor as the tributes that lie
at her chipped plaster hem. The keys and the beads and
      inhalers;
the opened lipsticks, their pressed-juice coloured flesh

all chalked in the rain. And I think what a furious place
is the heart: so raw, so pure and so shameless.
We both drink the water. I drink with defiance
and you drink without it. No one is watching, but God,
and He doesn't care, except for the heart's intention.
I think how to live. That I will take nothing, leave nothing.
That I will live lightly, as you do. Backwards, as this stone
      cross,
thinned and unwritten by centuries of weather.

Outside the Pale

Three nuns by the sea:
one held the shoes, the others
dropped shells into cupped hands.

It was better
when they wore the long crow habits.
Still it was fine

to see the holy sisters join the dance.
When we returned from our slow stroll
by the matte sea in the white light

they were sat in the grey dunes reading at thrillers —
feet stuck with sand, shoes lying out,
a mist of fine rain drifting.

The desk light in the winter dusk
making the usual pool, the shells
in fading muddle on the table. She fingers them,

the oatmeals and the creamy whites,
the fluted edges and the plum-stained chambers.
Pottery pieces, yellow-veined,

garland-swagged,
an oyster, its tide-marked carapace,
sea glass shaped

like a sound. It is
some other country. To be entered
like sorrow, and passed through.

Acknowledgements

Acknowledgements are due to the editors of the following publications where versions of many of these poems first appeared: *Agenda, Books Ireland, Crab Orchard Review, The Cúirt Journal, Force Ten, The Honest Ulsterman, The Observer Arvon Poetry Collection, The Poetry Business Anthology, Poetry Ireland Review, Spark, The Sunday Tribune, Tears in the Fence, The Waterford Review, Weyfarers* and *The Works*. A number of these poems appeared in 'In Sickness', HU Publications, 1995.

Thanks are due to the Tyrone Guthrie Centre at Annaghmakerrig.

The author wishes particularly to thank all at Lithos Road and at the Butler House.